I0450317

TABLE OF CONTENTS

IT'S NOT ROCKET SURGERY!
HOW TO LAUNCH, RATHER THAN DETONATE, YOUR CHILD.
OR, WHY SHOULD YOU TEACH YOUR CHILD TO READ BEFORE KINDERGARTEN

(This book is produced as a series, one chapter at a time. If you like this one, you'll love the next one. Each chapter will come with its own HELPS and Appendix full of ideas.)

8.   THE TEN O'CLOCK SCHOLAR – LEARNING STYLES

Keep your child from falling behind in school (public, private, or home).

Did you know that there are different learning styles? We've all heard of left-brained (sequential) and right-brained (spatial) learning. And we've all heard of auditory (hearing) or visual (seeing) learning. But there are a couple of more recent categories that link them together with more definition. Have you ever heard of auditory-sequential versus visual-spatial learning? (Highly gifted children often have both). Children, even gifted children, with visual-spatial learning may be misdiagnosed with learning disabilities. And what about late-bloomers?

For example – as I discussed in a previous chapter – one of my sons skated through elementary school with no problems, other than his mouth (gifted children often think their opinion *must* be heard). But in middle school, with multiple teachers and classrooms constantly changing, as well as more challenging subjects, he started to struggle. His problems increased in junior high, when he was diagnosed with both ADHD and depression. (I contend that makes him bipolar, but the psychiatrist says not.) He received *very* high scores on the ACT test without ever cracking a study guide, then failed 5 classes that trimester. Five. Go figure.

I now realize that my son is a visual-spatial learner. Most classrooms, lessons, and homework are geared towards audio-sequential learners. What's the difference? According to Dr. Linda Kreger Silverman, "Visual-spatial learners are individuals who think in pictures rather than in words. They have a different brain organization than auditory-sequential learners. They learn better visually than auditorally. They learn all-at-once, and when the light bulb goes on, the learning is permanent. They do not learn as well from repetition and drill. They are whole-part learners who need to see the big picture first before they learn the details. They are non-sequential, which means that they do not learn in the step-by-step manner in which most teachers teach. They arrive at correct solutions without taking steps, so 'show your work' may be impossible for them."

TAKE THIS QUIZ. What kind of learner are you?

AUDITORY-SEQUENTIAL	VISUAL-SPATIAL
Thinks primarily in words	Thinks primarily in pictures
Has auditory strengths	Has visual strengths
Relates well to time	Relates well to space
Is a step-by-step learner	Is a whole-part learner
Learns by trial and error	Learns concepts all at once
Progresses sequentially from easy to difficult material	Learns complex concepts easily; struggles with easy skills

Is an analytical thinker	Is a good synthesizer
Attends will to details	Sees the big picture; may miss details
Follows oral directions well	Reads maps well
Does well at arithmetic	Is better at math reasoning than computation
Learns phonics easily	Learns whole words easily**
Can sound-out spelling words	Must visualize words to spell them
Can write quickly and neatly	Prefers keyboarding to writing
Is well-organized	Creates unique methods of organization
Can show steps of work easily	Arrives at correct solutions intuitively
Excels at rote memorization	Learns best by seeing relationships
Has good auditory short-term memory	Has good visual long-term memory
May need some repetition to reinforce learning	Learns concepts permanently; is turned off by drill and repetition
Learns well from instruction	Develops own methods of problem-solving**

Learns in spite of emotional reactions	Is very sensitive to teachers' attitudes
Is comfortable with one right answer	Generates unusual solutions to problems
Develops fairly evenly	Develops quite asynchronously
Usually maintains high grades	May have very uneven grades
Enjoys algebra and chemistry	Enjoys geometry and physics
Learns languages in class	Masters other languages through immersion
Is academically talented or gifted	Is creatively, mechanically, emotionally, or technologically talented
Is an early bloomer	Is a late bloomer
This information is available in several publications including, *Upside-Down Brilliance: The Visual-Spatial Learner*, by Dr. Linda Kreger Silverman, DeLeon Publishing (Denver, 2002). http://www.gifteddevelopment.com	

**Here is where The Godfrey Method disagrees with Dr. Silverman. Even visual-spatial learners need phonics. More boys tend to be in the V-S category, yet they more often develop induced-dyslexia from whole-word reading methods than girls do. This is a proven scientific fact.

Even V-S learners need to start with TGM's unique picture-letters and system. TGM has children begin making words immediately with the first few sounds they learn, as in *A Pretty Girl Was Alpha Bette* and Chapters 1, 2, & 3 of this series. As they learn each new letter sound, children also sound out new words using all known letters so far. This gives your child a feeling of success in reading even before learning all 26 primary letter sounds, and gives visual-spatial learners the "bigger picture" while easily learning the details! Perhaps after having a good foundation in letter sounds, they readily leap to remembering whole words by sight, but without that underlying support, many flounder. See Section (d), below.

And child-led discovery does not work well in the elementary years. Children shouldn't have to 're-invent the wheel' every generation. Even visual-spatial learners do better with guidance from an adult. Too often we are enamored by theories that don't work well in practice. And remember, 'common sense' is not that common. Data over dogma, reason over rhetoric.

a)   Auditory-sequential learners.

The left brain-hemisphere is sequential, analytical, and time-oriented. Imagine my shock to learn that many girls and women are using more of the left side of their brain. So much for the myth of being 'illogical'. No wonder we like to analyze relationships with our girlfriends!

Auditory-sequential males would likely focus on the left side of their brain most of the time. But A-S females may have the added benefit of networking with their right side often. Hence, decorating the house with crafts and such. No, I am not saying one gender is better than the other, just diverse in processing. Problem-solving abilities are equal in men and women, though solutions may be approached differently. I saw this in the corporate world often.

Even auditory-sequential learners can benefit from hands-on learning. As discussed in Chapter 7, when I worked as a chemist on solid rocket motors (SRM), I volunteered every year to run several Expanding Your Horizons (EYH) workshops for middle school girls. To get them excited about math and science, my team taught the girls to make their own lotion with lab equipment. It was always one of the most popular workshops. There is nothing better for girls than to be mentored in math and science by successful women scientists and engineers. Plus I loved to show them my family picture with 14 children so they could see that they don't have to give up motherhood to use their brains, or vice versa. Mrs. Barton, my algebra teacher and mother of four, mentored me, and I want to pass her good example on.

b) Visual-spatial learners.

The right brain-hemisphere perceives the whole, synthesizes, and apprehends movement in space. More males tend to be visual-spatial learners. According to Linda Kreger Silverman, Ph.D., visual-spatial research has been "validated on 750 fourth, fifth and sixth graders. In this research, one-third [33%] of the school population emerged as *strongly* visual-spatial. An additional 30% showed a *slight* preference for the visual-spatial learning style. Only 23% were *strongly* auditory-sequential. This suggests that a substantial percentage of the school population would learn better using visual-spatial methods. [With TGM phonics!] [It also shows that about 53% of children learn fine from auditory-sequential learning. In fact, whole-language has caused *many* more problems than it has solved, if any.]

"Visual-spatial learners are individuals who think in pictures rather than in words. They have a different brain organization than auditory-sequential learners. They learn better visually than auditorally. They learn all-at-once, and when the light bulb goes on, the learning is permanent. They do not learn from repetition and drill. They are whole-part learners who need to see the big picture first before they learn the details. They are non-sequential, which means that they do not learn in the step-by-step manner in which most teachers teach. They arrive at correct solutions without taking steps, so 'show your work' may be impossible for them.

7

"They may have difficulty with easy tasks, but show amazing ability with difficult, complex tasks. They are systems thinkers who can orchestrate large amounts of information from different domains, but they often miss the details. They tend to be organizationally impaired and unconscious about time.

"They are often gifted creatively, technologically, mathematically or emotionally. You can tell you have one of these children by the endless amount of time they spend doing advanced puzzles, constructing with Legos, etc., completing mazes, counting everything, playing Tetris on the computer, playing chess, building with any materials at hand, designing scientific experiments, programming your computer, or taking everything in the house apart to see how it operates. They also are very creative, dramatic, artistic and musical.

"I'd like to share with you how the visual-spatial learner idea originated. Around 1980, I began to notice that some highly gifted children took the top off the IQ test with their phenomenal abilities to solve items presented to them visually or items requiring excellent abilities to visualize. These children were also adept at spatial tasks, such as orientation problems. Soon I discovered that not only were the highest scorers outperforming others on the visual-spatial tasks, but so were the lowest scorers.

"The main difference between the two groups was that highly gifted children also excelled at the auditory-sequential items, whereas children who were brighter than their IQ scores had marked auditory and sequential weaknesses. It was from these clinical observations and my attempt to understand both the strengths and weaknesses that the concept of the 'visual-spatial learner' was born."

Most public school classrooms are very one-sided, catering to the auditory-sequential learners. Both types of learning are necessary for well-rounded children. Children only have two brain hemispheres, and we are doing an excellent job teaching one of them (left). Visual-spatial children need a much different curriculum and probably even a different learning environment. When parents and teachers become more aware of how to teach the other (right) hemisphere, we will have happier students, learning more effectively.

c) Girls vs. boys.

It seems that these different learning styles also reflect, in general, the learning differences between girls and boys. Of course there are always exceptions, but girls tend to be more audio-sequential (left-brain), while boys tend to be more visual-spatial (right-brain). No wonder boys typically do better with 3-dimensional video games and girls generally enjoy writing more!

9

This is counter-intuitive to the original left-brain/right-brain theory of men vs. women, but explains why many boys don't catch up academically to girls until middle school age. I was always taught that men were more logical and left-brained, and women were more right-brained. Dr. Silverman's research shows, not necessarily. Perhaps the idea that men are more "logical" stems from the truth that it is more common for females to network both brain hemispheres simultaneously, whereas males tend to use one side at a time. Often men don't to understand the leaps that women make in connecting multiple data streams, therefore think they are illogical. Quite the opposite is true, actually.

Plus, socially it is more acceptable for women to express emotions, so they do. The emotions can still be based on intuitive logic, but misunderstood by men, who have learned to suppress most emotions in public (except anger). Both sexes feel the whole range of emotions, but their intensity and manifestation may differ. And what is important to males and females may be different, whether genetic, social, or both. Thus they can misinterpret each other's motivating factors. This does not mean one is more logical or emotional than the other. They complement each other.

Personally, I seem to have parts of both learning-styles: I learn better by seeing than hearing, *but* I am more sequential than spatial. Call me, visual-sequential, with a little of everything else thrown in.

10

There is an intriguing article by Sharon Begley, <u>Gray Matters</u>, *Newsweek* (March 27, 1995), at http://www.newsweek.com/1995/03/26/gray-matters.html. **Quoting several sections:**

"Of course men and women are different. Boy, are they different. In every sphere of life, it seems, the sexes act, react or perform differently. Toys? A little girl daintily sets up her dolls, plastic cups and saucers, while her brother assembles his Legos into a gun -- and ambushes the tea party. Navigating? The female tourist turns her map every which way but right, trying to find the way back to that charming bistro, while her boyfriend charges ahead, remembering every tricky turn without fail. Relationships? With spooky intuition, women's acute senses pick up subtle tones of voice and facial expressions; men are insensitive clods who can't tell a sad face until it drenches them in tears. Cognition? Females excel at language, like finding just the right words to make their husbands feel like worms; males can't verbalize even one good excuse for stumbling home at 2 a.m.

"Stereotypes? Maybe -- but as generalizations they have a large enough kernel of truth that scientists, like everyone else, suspect there's something going on here. As Simon LeVay, a Salk Institute neuroscientist put it recently, "There are differences in the mental lives of men and women."

"With new technologies like functional magnetic resonance imaging (FMRI) and positron emission tomography (PET), researchers catch brains in the very act of cogitating, feeling or remembering. Already this year researchers have reported that men and women use different clumps of neurons when they take a first step toward reading and when their brains are "idling." And, coming soon to a research journal near you, provocative studies will report that women engage more of their brains than men when they think sad thoughts -- but, possibly, less of their brains when they solve SAT math problems.

"Twenty-two male and 22 female students were PET-scanned while they solved SAT math problems. By detecting areas of the brain using the most blood, PET pinpoints active regions.

"Male students with high SAT scores showed intense activity in the temporal lobes (red spots at top and sides), compared with men with average scores. In men, it seems, ability is related to how hard the brain works.

"Brain activity in the mathematically gifted women was less intense than in the high-SAT men, even though their scores were comparable. These women expended no more neural effort than the average-SAT women.

Summarized from the PET Scan Photo:

- The region of the cerebral cortex that helps control hearing, memory and a person's sense of self and time, is stronger in men.

- Women have more neurons in a tiny region of the temporal lobe behind the eye, which understands language as well as melodies and speech tones. In cognitively normal men, this region has about 10 percent fewer neurons than it does in women.

- The bundle of neurons that is the main bridge between the left brain and the right, carrying messages between them is larger in men. (A bigger brain area matters only if it has more neurons, the cells that carry communications, in it. This is not yet proven.)

- In women, the back part of the callosum is bigger than in men. This may explain why women use both sides of their brain for language. A man's corpus callosum takes up less volume in his brain than a woman's does, suggesting the two hemispheres communicate less.

- In men, the commissure is smaller than it is in women, even though men's brains are, on average, larger than women's. The larger commissure in women may be another reason their two cerebral hemispheres seem to work in partnership on tasks from language to emotional responses.

"Women tend to have better language skills -- perhaps because the emotional right brain enriches their left-brain vocabulary. And women have better intuition -- perhaps because they are in touch with the left brain's rationality and the right's emotions simultaneously.

"Women can't understand why men find it so hard to be sensitive to emotions. According to the PET scans, women's brains didn't have to work as hard to excel at judging emotion. Women's limbic system, the part of the brain that controls emotion, was less active than the limbic system of men doing worse. That is, the men's brains were working overtime to figure out the faces. But the extra effort didn't do them much good.

"Men and women were asked whether the expressions on actors' faces were sad or happy and were monitored by PET scans as they decided"

"Men did as well as women -- 90 percent right -- in identifying happy male and female faces. But they were worse at sensing sad women. Overall, women were better able to judge facial expressions of both sexes. The PET scan showed their brains required less energy than the men's to decide.

14

"But if the first tantalizing findings are any clue, the research will show that our identities as men and women are creations of both nature and nurture. And that no matter what nature deals us, it is we -- our choices, our sense of identity, our experiences in life -- who make ourselves what we are."

Great article, right?! But some people may try to use such scientific data to prove one sex is superior over the other. The truth is, society needs both types of brains, male and female, to function well. Our need for men's single-minded focus and for women's networking abilities became obvious to me in a wonderful book, *Women's Diaries of the Westward Journey*, by Lillian Schlissel, Schocken Books (1992).

In her book the author gives the historical account of the United States' westward movement through the eyes of the women. Historians typically write from the men's journals and perspectives, but Schlissel's work showed a different side to seeking land in Oregon, following the California gold rush, or the Mormon exodus to the Salt Lake Valley, to name a few of the prospects that pulled pioneers westward. The viewpoint of pioneer women gave a much richer flavor to the decisions and approaches to leave everything behind.

Men sought the bigger picture, gold, land, religious freedom, with a one-track mind, and made sure the wagons, animals, tools, rifles, etc., were ready to go. Women saw the difficulties in the details of how to keep children safe, keep yeast-starter for bread dough alive, how to cook, how to find water, pack enough food, essentially take care of everyone's everything. They had no desire to leave their established, comfortable homes in the East to head into the unknown. They must have been terrified to imagine giving birth without a midwife in the middle of nowhere. What if their children fell under the horses' hooves or wagon wheels? What if they got sick? Most pioneer women would never have gone west if their husbands hadn't insisted. Yet they were the glue that held the journey together.

As I read these true stories, I realized that progress takes both men and women; men to fearlessly forge ahead, and women to make sure everyone is safe, nurtured and cared for. That does not mean that they are pigeon-holed in those roles; there is a lot of overlap as men and women help each other. But in general, men's brains, using one brain hemisphere – or the other – at a time, give them the ability focus on the end goal. Women's brains, using both hemisphere's simultaneously, give them the ability to keep track of the details of everyday life and families. Men may be more aggressive to confront problems, while women may be more willing to compromise. Both ways of thinking balance each other. Neither is superior. We should celebrate everyone's gifts and appreciate each contribution to the community and family as a whole. I am equally proud of my eight daughters and my six sons. All are encouraged to pursue whatever interests, talents, and vocations they enjoy.

Some quote studies saying that our genes make us who we are. But that's only part of the truth. Environment and our own free-will both play a big part in whom we choose to become. Our consciousness is more than just the genes in our DNA. In fact, we can choose to overcome our genetic tendencies. Dr. Stanton E. Samenow's book, *"Before It's Too Late – Why some kids get into trouble and what parents can do about it,"* reports many cases of mind-over-matter in juvenile delinquents and their siblings. Nature plays a part in our tendencies; nurture plays a large part in galvanizing them; but our choices *of how we respond to events* play an equal part in whether we solidify those tendencies or not. Of course, good nurturing can help guide our choices towards the positive.

http://www.amazon.com/Before-Its-Late-Stanton-Samenow/dp/0812916468

Health Day News reports that "it's not nurture or nature that determine a predisposition toward delinquent behavior in adolescents, it's the combination of the two," say researchers from the University of North Carolina-Chapel Hill. Genetics and social factors are tied to male delinquency: family, friends, and school all impact the expression of certain molecular variants.

The *American Sociological Review* points to three genetic polymorphisms that, when paired with social factors, can predict future serious and violent delinquency:

"While genetics appear to influence delinquency, social influences such as family, friends and school seem to impact the expression of certain genetic variants," said study author – Professor Guang Guo of North Carolina-Chapel Hill. "Positive social influences appear to reduce the delinquency-increasing effect of a genetic variant, whereas the effect of these genetic variants is amplified in the absence of social controls."

"Our research confirms that genetic effects are not deterministic," Guo added. "Gene expression may depend heavily on the environment."

http://health.usnews.com/health-news/family-health/brain-and-behavior/articles/2008/07/17/genetics-social-factors-tied-to-male-delinquency

As Begley said, "...no matter what nature deals us, it is we -- our choices, our sense of identity, our experiences in life -- who make ourselves what we are."

This is why dyslexia is not genetic but induced. Even if a child has hearing-processing difficulties or genetic tendencies for dyslexia (and related disorders), his exposures to parenting and/or teaching methods are the *most significant factors*. The physical problems and tendencies can be surmounted. Triggers for dyslexia (et al), such as noise pollution and sight-reading, can be avoided. Early reading the right way *erases* dyslexic tendencies.

d) When a learning disability is really as simple as learning style. (When learning style is mistaken for learning disability.)

John Holt's book, *Teach Your Own*, first introduced me to the idea that dyslexia is mis-diagnosed. The idea that children see letters as 3-dimensional objects came from him, as he proved that children are not *seeing* letters backwards. Research from Dr. Samuel Blumenfeld and others has shown that sight-words are the culprit. When our educational system took true phonics out of the classroom, it was a step backwards. Whole-language is the limiting hieroglyphic system, whereas phonics is the most progressive innovation of the centuries. It still is.

Gifted children are not truly ADHD, just bored and full of ideas and energy. Dyslexia is neither visual nor genetic. It is induced. Tendencies are never set in stone and can be overcome by environment and free will. Late-bloomers are not "slow", just flourishing at their own rate. In fact, they are often very bright.

Help your son break the gender gap in reading so his gift can shine. Did you know that there is a world-wide gender gap in reading, especially with whole language or sight-reading methods? Science has shown that boys are very different from girls in fetal development, emotional response, brain differentiation, and such. The multi-focus teaching methods above favor girls in academic achievement. However, when the single-focus approach of systematic phonics is used, the sex differences are eliminated, with the boys even outperforming the girls sometimes.

Chapter 3, and one of my articles in www.examiner.com, discussed the Visual Attention Span (VAS) Theory. VAS is the number of letters that can be held in short-term memory and, as children mature, their VAS increases. The more letters a student can hold in his or her short term memory, the better he or she will fare with whole language/balanced literacy methods (which involve a lot of memorization).

As I shared in Chapter 5, out of the VAS clinical practice has come the results that since boys mature more slowly than girls, boys tend to have lower VAS scores and do worse at reading in whole language/balanced literacy classrooms. But in systematic phonics classrooms, where children are required to process sounds as opposed to memorizing letters, VAS is not a factor and there is no gender gap. The creators of VAS Theory use systematic phonics, succeeding in

20

teaching 100% of their students to read, with data based on their study of more than 3000 children.

So, knowing that children often fall behind with whole-language or sight-reading methods, a wise parent will make sure that her son (or daughter) has systematic, synthetic phonics taught as his method of reading! Since reading is the foundation of everything else, he will have a much better chance to be his brightest self. Geek is Chic! [See section (f).]

On July 15, 2011, I was a guest on Vivienne McNeny's internet radio show – The Sociable Homeschooler – http://toginet.com/shows/thesociablehomeschooler/articles/2070. Among our several topics of conversation, we discussed late bloomers. I have several family members who seemed to drift aimlessly as young adults, but who became successful later in life. Never give up!

"It's never too late to become the person you might have been" George Elliott

Vivienne shared how one of her sons was a ball of energy who couldn't settle down long enough to concentrate on his assignments. Did she put him on Ritalin? No, she wisely helped him by writing his stories as he dictated them to her, giving him oral spelling tests while he engaged in other activities, read books and textbooks with him, etc. To some her son may have had a learning disability, but he was just a late bloomer, who is fine now. He's also very intelligent, which giftedness is often misdiagnosed as ADHD. Vivienne had the insight to help her son learn until he flourished at his own pace.

Sometimes dealing with a child's struggles can seem exhausting. The best way to beat mommy burn-out is to change the way we're thinking about a situation. It also helps to find out that we're not alone and others are coping with similar issues.

The internet makes it easy to find social groups with similar interests and experiences. Sites like www.meetup.com have just about any kind of group you want to join. Google can find any subject. Support of friends goes a long way to helping us carry on with joy.

I just love the poem, DON'T YOU QUIT:

When things go wrong, as they sometimes will,

When the road you're trudging seems all uphill,

When the funds are low and the debts are high,

And you want to smile, but you have to sigh,

When care is pressing you down a bit-

Rest if you must, but don't you quit.

Life is queer with its twists and turns,

As every one of us sometimes learns,

And many a fellow turns about

When he might have won, had he stuck it out.

Don't give up though the pace seems slow -

You may succeed with another blow.

Often the goal is nearer than

> It seems to a faint and faltering man;
>
> Often the struggler has given up
>
> When he might have captured the victor's cup;
>
> And he learned too late when the night came down,
>
> How close he was to the golden crown.

Success is failure turned inside out -

> The silver tint in the clouds of doubt,
>
> And you never can tell how close you are,
>
> It might be near when it seems afar;
>
> So stick to the fight when you're hardest hit -
>
> It's when things seem worst that you must not quit.

Author Unknown

http://www.thedontquitpoem.com/thePoem.htm

e) The mind-body connection. Kinesthetics.

We all have 5 senses: sight, hearing, touch, taste, and smell. Personally, I would call emotion a sixth sense because I often feel my emotions in my heart or chest area, as well as other parts of my body. Science calls it psycho-somatic, meaning that the mind affects the body (and vice versa). Some parents make the mistake of only focusing on one area of a child's intelligence, either academic or sports. Children need exposure to many types of learning to be well-rounded. All areas affect the mind. Mental, physical, emotional, social, and spiritual healths are inter-related and we should encourage them in our children, for robust lives and futures.

There is a mind-body connection that is important to understand. There are many examples of times when body movement optimizes mental ability. Since the goal of most parents is for their gifted children to be well-rounded people, the mind-body connection is important to consider.

There is a proven connection between academics, infants and academics. Crawling affects language, reading, and math abilities. Children who crawled longer as babies often have an increased ability to learn during school years. In fact, children who are struggling in school show marked improvement when they do crawling exercises each day, even at ten years old or older. The eye-hand-leg coordination that is learned helps brain processing in all areas. It may be related to spatial relationships and timing patterns, which always improve math and reading. Young parents are often excited to have their babies walking early, but wise parents will encourage their infants to crawl longer.

Playing an instrument such as piano improves mental functioning. Music definitely improves space and time understanding, which maximizes learning in all areas. Likewise, hearing classical music from Brahms, Bach, Beethoven, and Mozart has been proven to increase intelligence in infants and children. There is something about the compositions from these four geniuses that increase the necessary neuron paths required for higher-level thinking. Wise parents incorporate music into their children's lives, by both listening and playing instruments.

Playing sports can sharpen logic and logistical intelligence. Grasping how several players coordinate together, and all the many possibilities of interaction and play, is an important part of problem-solving later in life.

About age 5, it may be a good idea to start children in community t-ball, soccer, basketball or swimming. The recreation department at most city offices has information on all community sports. They also usually have a city pool that offers affordable swim lessons during the summer. Start children in sports early. The hand-eye-leg coordination required is akin to crawling in maximizing intelligence. Caution: do not neglect intellectual stimulation for physical prowess.

Three of my sons loved the swim team. None of them became Olympic or professional material, but they learned valuable lessons and strengthened their bodies, which strengthened their minds, and learned the value of teamwork. The oldest went to the State Swim Competition. Smart children are often independent and stand alone in their intellectual abilities. They may begin to think that their way is the only way, or that because they are smart, they are always right. It is good for them to learn teamwork and compromise in a team sport. It is good for them to learn that others have good ideas, too.

The steps to success are intention, attention, and then no tension. First, write down the goal that is intended to accomplish. Then give it attention and real effort for a sustained time. Finally, release the tension and do something else for awhile. It is while doing something physical that the "Aha!" moments often come.

Personally, I pace when I'm having a mind blank. Washing dishes, walking, exercising, creating something with your hands, or just doing something physical releases ideas from the mind at unexpected times. Sleep affects mental acuity, too. Some "Aha!" moments occur in the middle of the night, awakened from sleep, where the mind has had a chance to relax. Many geniuses relax with some sort of physical art like painting, sculpting, carpentry, or other creative activity unrelated to their area of expertise. Giving the conscious mind a break allows the subconscious to kick in ideas.

Chiropractors such as Dr. Bradley Nelson (*The Emotion Code*) have shown that stress stored in the body relates to memories of traumatic moments. There is also a strong correlation between depression and physical ailments, where a negative mental attitude suppresses the immune system and allows illness in. The reverse is also true, that chronic illness can provoke depression. Keeping a positive mental attitude can keep the body healthier. By the same token, proper nutrition and exercise keep the mind and emotions healthier.

Some parents make the mistake of only focusing on the gifted child's academic intelligence, or vice-versa. All other areas affect the mind, too. Mental, physical, emotional, social, and spiritual health are all inter-related and should be encouraged in gifted children for robust lives and futures.

"Mom, there's nothing to do!" Recognize that summer-time whine from your kids? Sometimes they need to put down the books, computer, and games and play outside. Children need the right side of their brains exercised as much as the left, so activities in the arts and humanities are refreshing and beneficial.

Stimulate your child's imagination and creative juices with family trips to local water parks, federal reserve banks, museums with activities, pioneer towns, skating, nature reserves and farmstead parks, puppetry institutes, children's science institutes, cave exploring, library activities, fine arts centers, community theaters, zoos, petting zoos, bird refuges, festivals, renaissances, college-sponsored math competitions for kids, picnics, nature hikes, arts & crafts, amusement parks, camping, historical sites, old downtown shops, reunions, to name a few.

Specialty museums, such as Native American museums and cultural centers, are a great way to expand your child's social understanding. Local history is a splendid way to open your child's mind to the past. Many historic buildings have tours and children's activities. Check them out!

f)   The brain needs constant data input.

Did you know that the brain needs constant data-input? An old proverb says that those with high intelligence talk about ideas, with middle intelligence talk about things, and with low intelligence talk about people. Those who can't entertain themselves in wholesome ways, such as reading, creating art, designing or engineering something, writing, recreational activities, etc., still need data-input.

Some tend to shop too much or redecorate their houses for the umpteenth time, gossip, pick fights, buy another pocket knife or tool, watch too much sports, primp in the mirror a lot, and so on. Their brains need new data-input all the time, but it tends to be on a very shallow level of immediate gratification without much thought. Quite often it's just visual input of things to look at for no real reason, such as television, internet, video games, or driving around. Moderation in all things is the key.

Astute parents will gear their child's data-input towards ideas and creativity. To ensure that a child develops higher-level thinking, first teach him/her to read early the right way and to love reading. Surround your child with books, artistic tools and building sets. Get the child a simple microscope set. Play board games and/or do puzzles together as a family. Encourage your child to find things to do that give quality data-input into the brain.

It is useful for a person to know how to make small-talk in social situations, but for the most part s/he needs the ability to discuss ideas and be creative. Data-input for the brain should be uplifting, creative, and challenging. Parents who help their children learn how to motivate and entertain themselves – and think without the constant need of outside entertainment – will raise flourishing, high-level thinkers and problem-solvers.

Being a geek is gaining not only acceptance but also popularity. I recently saw a t-shirt that said, "Geek is Chic." I loved it! Remember, geeks and nerds run the world. So, I decided to Google that wonderful phrase and came up with so many positive resources. Check these out!

- *The Chic Geek's Fashion, Grooming and Style Guide for Men*, Marcus Jaye, Sterling Pub Co Inc, 2011.
- *Geek Wisdom*, N.K. Jemisin, Random House Inc, 2011.
- *The Geek Dad Book for Aspiring Mad Scientists: The Coolest Experiments and Projects for Science Fairs and Family Fun*, Ken Denmead, Penguin Group USA, 2011.
- *Suck It, Wonder Woman!: The Misadventures of a Hollywood Geek*, Olivia Munn, St Martins Pr, 2010.
- *Theater Geek: The Real Life Drama of a Summer at Stagedoor Manor, the Famous Performing Arts Camp*, Mickey Rapkin, Simon & Schuster, 2010.
- *Geek Charming*, Robin Palmer, Puffin Books, 2009.
- There were so many more humorous and interesting titles and products!

In summary, encourage your child to focus on ideas and creativity for his/her brain data-input. It is possible to be a geek and still have social skills without being materialistic.

g) Reduce those power struggles over learning!

Here are some suggestions for taking the wind out of an argument's sail. Talk with children, not to them. Win cooperation – recognize a behavior's purpose; feel NO rancor; discuss.

USE SENTENCES LIKE:

- "How do _?"
- "You may be right."
- "We'll think about it and see what happens."
- "What can _?"
- "I wonder why _?"
- "What if _?"
- "What else could _?"
- "Do you have any ideas _?"
- "I would appreciate it if you would _."
- "I don't agree with you, but you have the right to think so, if you wish."

We can improve the way we think about things with a few simple suggestions. We can replace negative habits with positive ones, as suggested below. REPLACE:

- Resentment & Discontent with GRATITUDE
- Criticisms with COMPLIMENTS
- Anger with HUMOR, PATIENCE, WISDOM
- Selfishness with SERVICE
- Ridicule with RESPECT
- Error with REPENTANCE
- Cruelty with CHARITY
- Contention with PEACE
- Pride with HUMILITY
- Rudeness with COURTESY
- Worry with FAITH

"Life is not the survival of the fittest, but the fitting of as many as possible for survival." Thomas H. Huxley, ad-libbed.

Dr. Randy S. Chatelain, Chair of the Human Relations Department at Weber State University, developed the astute

OPPOSITIONAL VS. OPPORTUNITY SYSTEMS:

OPPOSITIONAL SYSTEMS versus By Dr. Randy S. Chatelain, Ph.D.	OPPORTUNITY SYSTEMS Weber State University
TRAITS OF THE OPPOSITIONAL SYSTEM "LIFE IS SEEN AS A FIGHT TO WIN"	TRAITS OF THE OPPORTUNITY SYSTEM "LIFE IS SEEN AS AN OPPORTUNITY TO GROW"
1. WIN-LOSE: If I let you win, I will lose.	1. WIN-WIN-WIN... I can win, you can win, and the relationship can win.
2. You are either ON MY SIDE or AGAINST ME.	2. There is ENOUGH OPPORTUNITY FOR EVERYONE.
3. VERTICAL... I must be Top Dog, Superior, or in Control.	3. HORIZONTAL... There is an ABSENCE OF JUDGING and rejection. Inadequacy is OK as growth is pursued.
4. MISTRUST of others or the system.	4. GROWTH MOTIVATED – I am highly motivated towards my growth and your growth, but not motivated against you.
5. I am RIGHT, and you are WRONG if you differ from me.	5. ENERGY IS NOT WASTED in OPPOSITION or JUDGING.
6. MANIPULATION and CONTROL using Sympathy, Duty, Rejection, Criticism, Threats, Conditional Approval, etc.	6. There are MULTIPLE PATHS OF GROWTH and BROAD DEFINITIONS OF SUCCESS.
7. INTELLIGENCE IS POWER to be superior, belittle, criticize, and control.	7. My purpose is to TOUCH THE LIVES OF OTHERS, as well as achieve my own growth and goals.
8. FAILURES ARE RECORDED IN DETAIL and long-term memory.	8. ONE plus ONE equals THREE $1+1=3$ Through cooperation, together we are more than either of us individually. Synergy.
9. HESITATION TO DEPEND ON OTHERS or to delegate; it may hold me back or slow me down.	9. I am thrust FORWARD if I take time and energy to HELP ANOTHER person.
10. LOCOMOTIVES and BRAKES... I must apply the brakes to your locomotive; take you down a notch.	10. PEACE and HARMONY are experienced when I let go of fighting myself, others, society, God, etc.

Which kind of relationships do you develop? It is possible to discipline without anger, with love and logic. Better late than never.

The Godfrey Method insists that parents de-fuse the control games by keeping the learning fun and stopping when young children are ready to take a break. Another way is to change your viewpoint of what it means to be the parent, the boss, the authority.

Without the preventatives shown in this chapter, the cracks in your child may be dyslexia, speech problems, resource remediation classes, being teased, attention-deficit hyperactivity disorder (ADHD), autism, low self-esteem, insecurity, childhood depression, low self-confidence, lack of imagination, lower IQ, slower learning capacity, poor decision-making skills, lack of social skills, math incompetency, low-paying jobs, and/or caught in the downward educational trend. They all may be preventable or curable. You, mom and dad, are the key. It's not rocket surgery!

HOME EARLY LEARNING PLAY SCHOOL (HELPS) 8 - Finding the Secret Codes for more diphthongs (vowel blends), consonant blends, homonyms, and exceptions. (A Handbook for Reading, blue). Spy Rules 26 – 35 (except 34 & 39 which are in Chapter 7). Phonics Charts 26-35 & 13b.

Why all these charts, you ask? Because organizing and categorizing help children remember words easier and make associations between spellings, pronunciations, and meanings!

Spy Game – The Secret Codes:

Spy Mission 8: Uncover the secret world of new letter blends which change the sounds. You (child) are the world-famous spy, Cody Breaker! Your eighth mission is to figure out which new letter blends have more than one sound, and when. You will crack the code of strange vowel sounds like 'war' and 'wor.' Many of these blended sounds are neither long nor short, so the mystery is yours to solve!

You can decipher this puzzle by figuring out the new Spy Code Rules. Find words around you that follow each rule. Great job. Spy out some more!

Use the Phonics charts 26-35, 13b & 17b, in the appendix, along with the books, if desired. Have mom or dad explain the examples on the Phonics Charts, if needed.

Have a scavenger hunt for the new blends in the signs, books, and the world around you. Report to the Spy Chief regularly about what you have found. Your next Spy assignment is to practice the alternate sounds often. On your paper, write words from the phonics charts in the appendix. Talk about the secret rules, below, of when to use which sounds, and find examples of each type. You're the right Spy for the job. You can do it!

Spy Tools:

Spy Chief, use phonics chart found in the appendix, with your child. You can start introducing the corresponding words as you present each concept with the Spy Code Rules 26-35. This will help your Spy know when alternate sounds are used for the new blends. A couple of the charts are review from previous chapters, but fit well in this group also. Note how interesting it is that adding 'w' to 'ar' and 'or' often changes the vowel sound!

You might not want to do all of them in one sitting. Have your little Spy search for new examples in books, signs, etc. Practice. Let your child practice matching alternate sounds to words and draw pictures to illustrate them, especially for the differences in homonyms (which spelling goes with which meaning).

- Have a scavenger hunt to find as many words as possible that have the consonant blends in Chart 26, below. Set a goal or see who can find the most. Do the same for all the 'er (ir, ur)' sounds in Chart 27.
- Play find-the-silent-letters in words from the charts. Have a point system and reward, if desired. See if you can spot words that have homonyms (not listed, here).
- Play find-the-rhyming words with words from the charts. Ask, what else rhymes with this word?
- Use index cards for each of these, if desired.

- Have a friendly spelling test after each Spy Rule & Chart review, orally and/or written. Be creative! Have joyous fun with it!
- Spy Chief, try this spelling game with your little Spy to strengthen his/her memory:
  - Spell 'rŭff' – rough.   The sandpaper was rough.
  - Spell 'thrū' – through.   We drove through the tunnel.
  - Spell 'thō' – though.   Though I love pizza, no thanks.
  - Spell 'therō' – thorough.   Be thorough when cleaning.
  - Spell 'tŭff' – tough.   This spelling test is tough.
  - Spell 'thou' – thou.   Thou art the Lord.
  - Spell 'cŏff' – cough.   He had a bad cough.
  - Spell 'bow' – bough.   A tree bough is fun to climb.
  - Spell 'cŏt' – caught.   She caught the ball.

The <u>Spy Code Rules</u>: (just practice one or two at a time, and search for examples in the charts and in words around you.)

Spy Code Rule 26: Consonant rule: two or more consonants can come together in a word to blend two or more sounds. See Chart 17b in Chapter 4.

Spy Code Rule 27: The ur rule: all three- er, ir, and ur say 'ūr' (fur).

Spy Code Rule 28: The or rule: or usually says 'ōr' (for), but after w it says 'ūr' (word).

Spy Code Rule 29: The all rule: all usually says 'ŏl' (ball).

Spy Code Rule 30: The ar rule: ar usually says 'ŏr' (car) like the *name* of the letter r, but after w it says 'ōr' (ward).

Spy Code Rule 31: The wa rule: when a comes after w, it can say 'ā' (wane), 'ă' (wax), 'ō' (war), 'ŏ' (want), or 'ŭ' (was).

Spy Code Rule 32: The a- rule: when a comes in front of a two-syllable word, it usually says 'ŭ' (alone).

Spy Code Rule 33: The ie rule (silent i for long e rule): usually put i before e (relieve, field, friend), except after c (receive, receipt), unless it says 'ā' (neighbor, weigh). Exceptions: stein, society, etc. See Chart 13b from Chapter 6.

Spy Code Rule 35: dge (and ge) say the *soft* g sound at the end of a word. gue in a word says the *hard* g sound.

Spy Code Book:

      The Spy Code Book is the charts found below in the appendix. The Spy Chief must follow it for optimum mission success.

Spy Reporting:

      Show your Spy (child), Cody Breaker, how to report what s/he has found by writing down the alternate sounds that s/he has found so far. And/or practice a few from Charts 26-35 in the appendix. To truly understand the code, s/he must master writing the code him/herself. Using the computer keyboard is not enough. Writing by hand strengthens the mind and ability to remember things, as well as eye-hand coordination. Practice two or three words from the charts for each rule, per session, or more if the child desires.

      Use the Century Gothic font (lower-case) as your letter-shape guideline. For example, A B C D E F G H I J K L M N O P Q R S T U V W X Y Z, matching with a b c d e f g h i j k l m n o p q r s t u v w x y z, is the easiest style to learn to write. Remember to print each letter in its left-to-right sequence, and in its proper bottom-to-top or top-to-bottom orientation, like cursive does, as explained in the Chapter 1 HELPS. Use lined paper.

      Help your little Spy enjoy making and looking for the alternate sounds in words. Keep It Simple For Success (KISS your child). Reward his/her efforts regularly; a hug, a pat, a bit of praise, a treat, a privilege. Encouragement goes a long way. Keep it happy!

APPENDIX

HELPS – ACTION PLANS – SPY CODE CHARTS

Phonics Charts 26-35, 13b & 17b.

Phonics Chart 26 (17b): Consonant blends ~ found at beginnings and/or ends of words. Most can be found in middles of words, too. Review from Chapter 4.

Consonant Blends & Blend:	Word-location:	Examples:
ck	end	back, luck
ght	end	right, ought
ks	end	ranks, forks
lb	end, middle	bulb, album
lc	end, middle	talc, falcon
ld	end	gold, bald
lf	end	elf, shelf
lk	end	milk, bulk
lm	end	calm, film
lp	end	scalp, pulp
ls	end	fills, boils
lt	end	colt, fault
mb	end	comb, lamb
mn	end	column, hymn
nd	end	sand, kind
nt	end	bent, pant
rb	end	curb, suburb
rc	end	arc
rd	end	yard, bird
rf	end	surf, turf
rg	end	iceberg, burg

rk	end	cork, park
rl	end	curl, snarl
rm	end	worm, farm
rn	end	horn, yarn
rp	end	harp, burp
rs	end	cars, hers
rt	end	fort, part
ts	end	bats, hits
bl	start	blend, black
br	start	broom, brave
cl	start	close, clever
cr	start	crop, crumb
dr	start	drip, dram
dw	start	dwell, dwarf
fl	start	flop, flame
fr	start	fruit, fresh
gl	start	glad, glory
gr	start	grow, great
kl	start	klutz, Klondike
kr	start	krylon, krill
pl	start	place, plot
pr	start	proud, prince
rh	start	rhyme, rhythm
sc	start	scat, scare
sl	start	slip, slack
sn	start	snack, snore
sp	start	spine, sport

squ	start	squeal, squeeze
str	start	strap, strong
sv	start	svelte, Svengali
sw	start	swell, swift
tr	start	truth, trip
tw	start	twelve, twins
wh	start	whale, which
wr	start	wrong, write
ch	start/end	chat, such
gh	start/end	ghost, tough
ly	start/end	lyrics, truly
ph	start/end	phone, graph
sh	start/end	short, mash
sk	start/end	skill, risk
sm	start/end	smile, chasm
st	start/end	stop, most
th	start/end	thin, with
sr	start	sro, Sri Lanka
tch	end	match, notch
spl	start	splash, split

Phonics Chart 27: The ur rule: all three - er, ir, and ur - say 'ūr' (fur).

er	except.'s	ir	ur	ur
berg	earth	bird	burr	purl
certain	learn	birth	blurb	purple
clerk	pearl	birthday	burger	purse
derf	search	chirp	burka	slurp
fern	yearn	dirt	burl	surf
germ		fir	burn	surge
her	journal	firm	burp	turn
herb		first	burst	
jerk		gird	churn	
kernel		girl	curb	
mermaid		girth	curd	
nerve		mirth	curfew	
per		shirk	curl	
perk		shirt	curse	
serve		sir	curt	
stern		skirt	curve	
term		stir	fur	

terse		swirl	furl	
verb		third	gurgle	
verse		thirst	hurl	
		virtue	hurt	
			jury	
			nurse	
			purge	

Phonics Chart 28: The or rule: or usually says 'ōr' (for), but after w it says 'ūr' (word).

ōr	ōr	ōr	ōr	er, ir, ur
bōrder	fōrth	nōrthern	spōrt	word
bōrn	hōrn	pōrk	stōre	work
cōrk	hōrse	pōrt	stōrm	world
cōrn	lōre	scōrcher	tōre	worm
cōrner	mōre	scōre	tōrn	worse
doōr	<except>	poōr	vōrtex	worth
fōr	mōrning	scōrn	**wōre**	< except
fōrk	nōr	snōrt	**wōrn**	< except
fōrk	nōr	sōre	yōre	
fōrt	nōrth	sōrt		

Phonics Chart 29: The all rule: all usually says 'ŏl' (ball).

Otherwise, 'all' follows the double-consonant/short-vowel (Spy Code 39) rule.

ŏl		ăl		ŭl
äll		ălley		allow
bäll		ălly		
cäll		băllet		
fäll		căllous		
gäll		dălly		
häll		găllows		
mäll		hăllow		
ställ		săllow		
täll		shăll		
wäll		tăllow		
wällow	**älready**	vălley		

Phonics Chart 30: The ar rule: ar usually says 'är' (car) like
the *name* of the letter *r*, but after w it says 'ōr'
(ward).

är	är	är	ōr
bär	jär	stärt	war
bärk	lärd	tär	ward
bärn	lärk	tärnish	warn
cär	märk	tärt	warning
cärd	märt	värnish	warp
därt	pärk	**wärm**	< except
fär	pärt	yärn	wart
färm	spärk		quart
gärnish	stär		quartz
härm	stärk		

Phonics Chart 31: The wa rule: when 'a' comes after 'w', it
can say 'ā' (wane), 'ă' (wax), 'ō' (war), 'ŏ' (want),
or 'ŭ' (was).

Phonics Chart 32: The a- rule: when 'a' comes in front of a two-syllable word, it usually says 'ŭ' (alone).

ŭ	ŭ	ŭ	ŭ
abed	ahoy	arose	accord
ablaze	ajar	around	affix
aboard	alike	asleep	allow
about	alive	aver	annoy
above	alone	avoid	apparel
afraid	along	avow	arrest
again	aloud	awake	assist
aghast	amass	aware	assort
ago	amount	awash	assume
agree	anoint	away	attain
ahem	apart	awoke	attempt
			attract

Phonics Chart 33 (13b): Silent Letters – Changing Short Vowels to Long Ones with Silent "i" plus Homonyms & Exceptions. Chapter 6 review.

Silent i for long ē rule: i before e, except after c*; unless it says ā, as in neighbor & weigh. (Except German stein, etc.)			
Examples:	**believe**	*deceive	
	relieve	*receive	
	cĕll	*cēiling	
sĕptic	accĕpt	*recēipt	

Short ĕ Vowels	Long ē Vowels	Homonyms	
mĕn	**miēn**	mēan	
lĕns	**liēns**	lēans	
chĕf	**chiĕf**		
thĕft	**thiĕf**		
pĕr	**piĕr**	pēēr	
prĕss	**priēst**		
tĕrm	**tiēr**	tēar	
Long ī Vowels	Long ē Vowels	Homonyms	
nīce	**niēce**	knēēs	
spīce	**piĕce**	pēace	
prīze	**priēst**		
Short Vowels	Long Vowels	Homonyms	
fĕll	**fiēld**	filled	Long e + l can sound like short i + ll.
shĕll	**shiēld**	shilled	
yĕll	**yiēld**		

Phonics Chart 35: dge (and ge) say the *soft* g sound at the end of a word. gue in a word says the *hard* g sound.

Soft g	Soft g	Hard g	Hard g
abridge	hedge	ague	plague
acknowledge	hedgehog	analogue	prologue
badge	hodge	argūe	rogue
badger	podge	baguette	segué
bridge	judge	beleaguer	segue
budge	knowledge	brogue	synagogue
budget	ledge	catalogue	tongue
cartridge	lodge	colleague	travelogue
codger	midge	daguerre-otype	vague
cudgel	midget	demagogue	vogue
curmudgeon	nudge	dialogue	
didgeridoo	partridge	epilogue	
dislodge	pledge	fatigue	Note: several -logue words are now spelled without the ue at the end, such as:
dodge	porridge	guernsey	
dredge	pudgy	guerrilla	
drudge	ridge	guess	
edge	sedge	guest	
fidget	sledge	harangue	
fledge	sludge	intrigue	analog
fledgling	smidgen	league	catalog
fridge	stodgy	meringue	dialog
fudge	trudge	monologue	epilog
gadget	wedge	morgue	monolog
grudge	widget	pedagogue	prolog

MOTTOS OF THE GODFREY METHOD

1. Keep It Simple for Success (KISS your child) with The Godfrey Method

2. Top Ten Myths of Reading

3. Dress Your Child's Mind for Success

4. Early Reading the Right Way – The Godfrey Method

5. Reading is Hearing with Your Eyes

   Phonics, phonics, phonics!

6. The Two Most Crucial Things Kids Need – Parent Time and Reading Skills

   Give quality parent time and excellent reading skills together with The Godfrey Method.

7. To Fix Public Education, Change What We're Teaching the Teachers to Teach.

   Removing faulty teaching methods must start in our universities (or at home).

   Second, we must change what methods are legislated into mandatory state curricula.

8. Nurture Your Child's Nature and Notions

   Intelligence is one-part nature, one-part nurture, and one-part inner-motivation.

9. "No Child Left Behind" has become All Children Left Behind

   Each term, curricula are readjusted (dumbed-down) to the slowest children.

10. It Doesn't Matter How the Child Makes You Feel; It Only Matters How You Make the Child Feel

    Remember, you're the adult.

11. Geeks and Nerds Run the World

    Think Bill Gates & Alan Greenspan, doctors, engineers, scientists, and inventors.

    Proud to be a geek!

12. Brains Always Beat Muscles

    Like pirates always beat ninjas (ask a gamer...)

13. Reverse Darwinism - Not Passing on Your Genes; Decline of the Fittest

    (When educated people choose NOT to have children and snuff out their genetic line.

    Centuries of survival now end with them. Dumbing-down of the world...)

14. Dyslexia is Induced – It's the Disease You Get from Sight-Reading

www.ingramcontent.com/pod-product-compliance
Lightning Source LLC
Chambersburg PA
CBHW070225290526
45789CB00004B/1515